MATT CHRISTOPHER®

On the Halfpipe with...

Tony Hawk

MATT CHRISTOPHER®

On the Halfpipe with...
Tony Hawk

Text by Glenn Stout

LITTLE, BROWN AND COMPANY
New York ᦇ An AOL Time Warner Company

First Edition

Matt Christopher® is a trademark of Catherine M. Christopher.

Cover photograph by Grant Brittain

Library of Congress Cataloging-in-Publication Data

Stout, Glenn.
　　On the halfpipe with — Tony Hawk / text by Glenn Stout. — 1st ed.
　　　　p.　　cm.
　　ISBN 0-316-14223-9 (pb)
　　1. Hawk, Tony — Juvenile literature.　2. Skateboarders — United States — Biography — Juvenile literature.　[1. Hawk, Tony. 2. Skateboarders.]　I. Title: Tony Hawk　II. Title.
GV859.8 .S86　2001
796.22'092 — dc21
[B]　　　　　　　　　　　　　　　　　　　　　　　00-056687

10　9　8　7　6　5　4　3

COM-MO

Printed in the United States of America

Contents

Chapter One:

Accidental Champion, Accidental Sport

Once upon a time, people thought skateboards were toys. And they believed that kids who rode skateboards were wasting their time.

Wrong!

Skateboard legend Tony Hawk changed those perceptions. Almost by himself, he turned skateboarding from a misunderstood pastime into a bona fide sport. Called by some the Michael Jordan or Babe Ruth of skateboarding, Hawk's inventive, athletic boarding style helped bring skateboarding into the mainstream of the sporting world. Widely acknowledged as the greatest skater of all time, Hawk is responsible for creating over *fifty* separate and unique skateboard maneuvers and turning an activity once considered a fad into a high profile, billion-dollar sport that attracts millions of skaters and fans all over the word. A generation ago, the notion that skateboarding would someday be one of the hottest sports in the world would have sounded absurd. Today, skateboarding is huge and Tony Hawk is a household name who has earned millions of dollars.

And it all happened by accident. Skateboarding wasn't created by some corporation, and its popularity isn't the result of some marketing plan. And when Tony Hawk first climbed onto a skateboard, he wasn't trying to be famous or thinking about making money by riding his board. He just wanted to have fun, like the millions of skaters who have followed in his wake.

The skateboard wasn't invented; it evolved. Ever since the invention of the wheel, human beings have experimented with different ways of locomotion. The skateboard is simply one of the more interesting and fun ways that people have devised to go from one place to another on wheels.

In the early 1800s a company in Chicago started putting wheels on shoes, creating the sport of rollerskating. But there was just one problem with roller skates: Growing kids quickly outgrew their skates.

Rather than throw the skates away, some inventive parents and their kids started taking the wheels off outgrown roller skates and attaching them to small carts, crates, and wagons. Kids rode these carts down hills and city streets.

But kids, being kids, weren't always satisfied with sitting in the carts. Some daring riders tried standing up in their carts and riding upright. Thus the skateboard, although no one thought to call it that, was born.

Boarding remained an accidental sport for much of the next one hundred years, although one variation, the scooter, began to be manufactured. Scooters were made of a metal or wooden plank with wheels and an upright handlebar to help the rider stand up and steer. Riders either rode downhill or gained speed on flat surfaces by pushing themselves forward with one foot and then gliding. It was fun, but scooters weren't very maneuverable. There was a limit to what a person could do on a scooter.

Meanwhile, missionaries to the Hawaiian Islands discovered that natives rode the surf on long planks of wood, which were later called surfboards. They carved the boards from trees, then stood upright on the boards and used the power of waves to propel them across the surface of the water. They crouched down and tilted their bodies to turn the boards and take advantage of the energy created by waves. In the early part of the twentieth century surfing came to the United States mainland. The sport took hold in California, and by the 1930s thousands of people were surfing the waves at California beaches.

But during certain times of the year in certain places along the California coast, the waves are too small for surfing. So surfers, many of whom recalled making their own carts and scooters with roller-skate wheels, started to take the same concept of wheeled transportation and apply it to a surfboard.

Through trial and error, they eventually came up with a scaled-down version of a wheeled surfboard that allowed the rider to mimic many of the same moves used while surfing. They started with a narrow plank of wood two or three feet long and less than a foot wide, shaped like a miniature surfboard. They attached roller-skate wheels to each end of the board. Riders discovered that not only did their invention allow them to roll across the ground at high speed, but that by leaning to one side or another they could steer and do other simple tricks. The first riders showed off by riding down streets that led to the beach, carving back and forth down the road like a slalom skier. When the waves returned, the extra practice helped them surf better.

In the 1950s a toy manufacturer created the Little Red Roller Derby, the first mass-produced skateboard, which consisted of a pair of steel wheels attached to each end of a plywood board. These were a big improvement on the homemade boards favored by the street surfers. Over the next ten years other manufacturers improved on the design and created their own versions, including one that was called the Sidewalk Surfboard.

Sidewalk surfboarding became a minor craze in California and spread to other parts of the country, where it was impossible to surf on water. At the time, surf music was a popular rock-and-roll style, and the sidewalk surfboard allowed people who had never seen the ocean to pretend they were surfers. Sidewalk surfing required only a board, a sidewalk, and some imagination.

In 1964 the California rock-and-roll duo Jan and Dean had a hit with a song called "Bust Your Buns (and Go Sidewalk Surfin' with Me)." The popular song turned the sport into a fad that swept the country.

Surfboard manufacturers jumped in and started creating their own sidewalk surfboards. Instead of using steel wheels, they began to use clay wheels similar to those used on roller skates, and the term "sidewalk surfboarding" came to be replaced by "skateboarding." Although the clay wheels weren't quite as durable as steel, they had better traction on pavement and gave the skater greater control. In just a few years, over fifty million boards were sold, primarily to kids.

As with many youth fads, adults just didn't understand the attraction to the sport. The reasons are varied and complex.

Part of the reason some people reacted with hostility toward skateboarders stems from the sport's close ties to surfing. The media coined the term "surf bum" in the 1950s to describe people who were perceived to spend all their time surfing. Nonsurfers, who often had a hard time telling one surfer from another, thought all surfers lived on the beach and didn't work.

While that stereotype may have been true for a

few surfers, most surfers were just like everybody else. They held jobs and had families but simply chose to spend most of their free time doing what they loved to do.

When skateboarding developed, many people assumed that skaters adhered to a similar stereotype. But stereotyping lumps different people together just because they share a few characteristics, and is rarely accurate. Like surfers, skateboarders come from all walks of life. Anybody who is willing to put in enough time practicing can be a skateboarder. It doesn't matter how you look or dress or behave.

Another reason a lot of non-skaters looked down on skateboarders is because people tend to be afraid of something new they don't understand. And to many people, skateboarding is *still* something new. Watching someone zip by on a skateboard is frightening to some people, particularly when a skateboarder cuts too close to a pedestrian on the sidewalk or darts between cars out into the street. As a result, the public often looks at all skateboarders the same way, even those who skate responsibly.

Because the sport looks dangerous, and a few

skateboarders don't respect the rights of others, since the 1960s some communities have made skateboarding illegal. In 1965, a cover story in *Life* magazine deemed the sport a "menace," and dozens of towns and cities banned skaters from their streets and sidewalks.

But laws have never stopped skaters from skateboarding. In the early years of the sport, there was no place but the street and sidewalk to skateboard. Yet because some skaters flouted the prohibitions against their sport, all skateboarders got stereotyped as juvenile delinquents and outlaws who had no respect for authority. As Tony Hawk later explained, "I think a lot of the outlaw image just stemmed from the lack of a place to skate."

Still, the first prohibitions against the sport led many serious skaters to stop skating, and kept nonskaters from taking up the sport. Surfers even began to distance themselves from skateboarding. And despite the improvements to the boards themselves, it was still almost impossible to do anything but glide along making sweeping turns. If a skater tried to turn quickly or make any other kind of tricky maneuver, the board tended to shoot out from under the rider and leave him flat on his back, nursing scrapes and bruises. And besides, the clay wheels didn't last long on rough pavement. They had to be replaced often and weren't widely available. So as quickly as the craze had started, it stopped. Skateboarding appeared to be dead, another temporary fad like the Hula-Hoop. By 1970 hardly anyone was riding skateboards anymore.

But in the mid-1970s, advances in roller-skate technology brought the sport back from the brink of extinction. Roller-skate manufacturers began experimenting with wheels made of urethane, a hard plastic that has better traction than either steel or clay wheels and doesn't wear out very quickly.

While serious roller-skaters disliked the new wheels, which they felt slowed them down, some skateboarders took their old skateboards out of the basement and attached the new roller-skate wheels to them. Modern skateboarding was born.

The skaters soon discovered that the new wheels allowed them to do things on a skateboard they'd only dreamed of before. The new wheels held to the ground during turns and rolled over small imperfections on the pavement without skidding, cracking, or becoming pitted and rough. Now riders could go fast and make sharp turns without falling or losing speed.

Manufacturers soon took note and began making skateboards with the new urethane wheels. Throughout the 1970s they experimented with various board and wheel designs. They made boards of varying lengths and widths out of fiberglass, plastic, aluminum, and wood. They added features like ball bearings and small suspension systems to the wheels and the skate trucks, the steel mounting system on the bottom of the board that attaches it to the wheels. Wheels were made in every possible combination of urethane and rubber, ranging from flat, smooth wheels to wheels with treads, and even some that were shaped perfectly round, like a ball. Skateboarders themselves even began lending their experience and expertise to the manufacturers. A few began manufacturing skateboards themselves.

Innovations in the sport came quickly. Although wood eventually became the preferred material for the board itself, manufacturers experimented with boards of varying lengths and widths built for different skating styles. The kicktail, a molded concave curve at the rear of the board, became a standard feature that allowed riders to place their weight behind the back wheels and made the board easier to control. Other skaters started adding high-traction surfaces like grip tape and other adhesives to the top of the board, and some even added Velcro straps that made it easier for the rider to maintain balance. They added plastic noses, tails, and rails to the boards to counteract wear and make it possible to slide or grind the edge of the board along sidewalk and curb edges.

All these changes enabled skaters to do things on a board that had been impossible before. Some skateboarders discovered that it was possible to skate in empty or abandoned swimming pools, making use of the steep, bowl-shaped, concrete surface to do things no one on a skateboard had ever thought of before.

One such skater was a thirteen-year-old boy named Alan Gelfand, whom his friends had nicknamed "Ollie." Gelfand, who lived in Florida, discovered an abandoned swimming pool in his neighborhood and spent hours skating back and forth, up and down its sides. He discovered that if he crouched down on his board as he went back and forth, he could eventually gain enough speed going down one side that he could pop upright and into the air on the opposite side. He practiced every opportunity he had, and soon could pop his board up in the air with his back foot, hold it steady with his front foot, and fly through the air while the board appeared stuck to his feet. In time, he discovered that he could even perform the trick on flat surfaces.

The move became known as the "Ollie." The Ollie, which today is one of skateboarding's most basic moves, changed skateboarding forever. Quite literally, skateboarding began to take flight.

When Alan Gelfand was developing the Ollie, Tony Hawk was only nine years old. He didn't even know what a skateboard was yet.

Chapter Two:

Skating By

As skateboard production became a big business in the mid-1970s, manufacturers soon began looking for ways to promote their product. They took note of how many kids were skating and decided to hold competitions, hoping to stimulate more interest in the sport and sell even more skateboards.

All sorts of competitions began to be held, ranging from timed speed races and slalom races down streets, to cross-country races along flat surfaces, to barrel jumps in which riders went down ramps and then jumped for height and distance. Skateboard makers even sponsored arena shows, similar to the Ice Follies or Ice Capades, where skateboarders wore costumes and skated to music.

But all these competitions imitated other sports, like skiing and ice-skating. A lot of skaters weren't

13

interested in those organized sports, and the competitions didn't really reflect the way most skaters used their skateboards. Many skaters were attracted to skateboarding because of the freedom of movement it allowed and its focus on individual expression.

The most popular forms of competition quickly became those that recognized that most skaters were different from many other athletes. Both freestyle and vert competitions catered to the kind of skating most kids did while fooling around on the streets and sidewalks and in abandoned swimming pools.

Freestyle, or street skating, is essentially a trick competition that mimics many of the conditions skaters face on the street. Skaters perform tricks while jumping curbs and do other tricks on railings and other common street obstacles. Freestylers put together routines of about a minute and try to do a large number of tricks that are judged according to their difficulty and style.

Vert skating developed from skaters who first started skating in swimming pools. Since there weren't very many pools, and it was usually illegal to skate in someone's pool, anyway, people began building structures of wood or concrete that resembled the high curved walls of the pool. They created halfpipes, ramps that look like big half circles, like lengths of pipe cut in half. Vert competitions last fifty seconds, and skaters are judged on the difficulty of their tricks, with the focus more on individual tricks than a sustained routine.

The manufacturers put a lot of money into the sport, trying to make it more popular. Some top skaters were even able to turn pro, earning money in competition and by giving sponsored clinics and demonstrations. Skating began to get big very quickly.

But just like the 1960s, some people still didn't understand what skating was all about. Skaters whizzing by pedestrians or in and out of traffic still frightened people unfamiliar with the sport. They thought the skaters were out of control. Once again, a number of communities banned skating in public places.

But now skating was too big a business to go away. In response to the prohibition of public skating, some communities and private developers began building skate parks, clusters of massive concrete or wood sculptures of halfpipes, bowls, curbs, ramps, and other features that mimicked the pools and public spaces where skaters loved to skate. Although many skaters still preferred to skate on the streets, skate parks provided a much-needed outlet for their talents, particularly in communities where public skating was banned. In just a few years over two hundred such parks opened.

But just as quickly as the skate parks had opened, many began to close. Several skaters had bad accidents in the parks and sued the operators, who had to pay thousands of dollars in damages. As a result, insurance companies stopped providing park operators with insurance, or charged exorbitant fees. In response, many park operators, afraid of being wiped out by lawsuits, closed their parks. Those that remained open charged skaters a lot of money to skate. The only recourse skaters had was to take to the streets and sidewalks again. But they still frightened people who didn't understand the sport, and more municipalities banned skateboarding on public byways. Skateboarding, for the second time, began to recede as a sport.

But in Carlsbad, California, just as many skaters were beginning to give up on the sport, one young boy was just getting started.

Tony Hawk was born in Carlsbad, about twenty miles north of San Diego, on May 12, 1968. His father, Frank, was a salesman and his mother, Nancy, an instructor at a community college. They had three much older children, daughters Lenore and Pat, who were already adults and living away from home, and an adolescent son, Steve.

Both his parents were in their early forties when Tony was born. Just a few months before his birth, his father had a heart attack and nearly died. Frank, who had served in both World War II and the Korean War as a pilot, soon recovered, but after his close call he decided to spend as much time as he could with his children.

"I probably spent more time with the kids than I should have," he said later. "But if they were into something that wasn't harmful, we tried to support it." But of the four Hawk children, Tony would prove to be his parents' greatest challenge.

Even when he was a toddler, Tony was full of energy. He just didn't know how to direct it. Hawk

17

later told reporters, "Instead of the terrible twos, I had a terrible youth. I was a hyper, rail-thin geek on a sugar buzz. . . . If I were growing up today they'd probably say I had attention deficit disorder," a common behavioral disorder.

He wasn't a bad kid; he just had so much energy he was constantly getting into trouble. Nancy Hawk later characterized him as "challenging . . . a very intense child, difficult and stubborn and hard to handle."

Yet Tony also occasionally displayed amazing focus and concentration for a young boy. When he was six years old he learned to swim, and became determined to swim the length of an Olympic-sized swimming pool underwater while holding his breath. He tried over and over again but kept failing. His mother had to drag her very frustrated and angry son back home.

As she later said, "He was so hard on himself, he expected to do so many things." When Tony started school, his parents began to worry because he became frustrated so easily. They finally took him to a psychologist to be tested.

The results were surprising. The Hawks were told their young son was "gifted"; he had a high IQ and was capable of doing schoolwork several grade levels above his classmates. One of the reasons he became so easily frustrated was due to the simple fact that he was bored. The psychologist described him as having "a twelve-year-old mind in an eight-year-old body." He explained, "His mind tells him to do things his body can't do."

Tony was immediately placed in advanced classes, which provided him with a challenge and kept him from becoming so bored. His parents also took him to violin lessons and encouraged Tony to play sports, hoping that physical exercise would channel his extra energy and improve his concentration. He started playing both basketball and baseball. Frank was very involved in his son's life, coaching Little League and practicing with him whenever Tony wanted.

Although Tony soon dropped his violin studies, he liked playing both baseball and basketball. But the enforced discipline of organized sports grated on him. He hated sitting on the bench while others played or waiting around during practice while performing some drill. He lacked patience and just wanted to play.

His older brother, Steve, was a serious surfer, a skill he eventually parlayed into a job editing a magazine devoted to surfing. Tony looked up to Steve, and one day when Tony was nine years old, Steve, who had just acquired a skateboard, encouraged Tony to jump on and take a ride. "You should try this," he said.

Tony stepped tentatively onto the board, standing sideways with his left foot in front, then pushed off carefully with his right foot, quickly putting it on the back of the board as he began to move. Tony struggled to maintain his balance as the board rattled slowly along the pavement, wheels whirring. As Tony rolled away, he called out to his brother, "How do I turn this thing?" Steve laughed and gave his little brother a few pointers.

A few moments later, Tony tumbled off the board for the first time, falling backward hard as it shot out from under him. But he got right back up and on the board. He had already decided that he loved skateboarding.

One of the reasons he liked it was because it was hard for him to do. In order to stay upright, he had to concentrate. When he did, all his problems and worries melted away. In comparison, when he played other sports his attention wandered when play slowed down. Then, when something happened, he often wasn't prepared and was slow to react, making him look bad.

He also loved the freedom he felt while riding on a skateboard and the fact that his success or failure was entirely dependent upon his own abilities. In skateboarding there were no time-outs, no fields or courts marked by lines, and no rules to learn and follow. The sport started the instant he stepped on the board, and continued until he stepped off. Tony quickly learned that his own talent and imagination — plus gravity and the laws of physics — were the only restrictions on where he could skate and what he could do on a skateboard.

Tony reveled in the feeling of independence and control he experienced on a skateboard. "I just liked being freer," he told a reporter years later, "not having to submit to some practice schedule of repetitive passing and shooting, and having to rely on other players in order to do well. There's a lot of practice in skateboarding, but it's at your own pace. That was the bottom line. I just didn't want to be ordered around."

Tony Hawk didn't know it yet, but his life was about to change forever. So was the sport of skateboarding.

Chapter Three:

Skateboard Little League

Tony soon got his own skateboard and began spending most of his free time learning to stay upright and do simple maneuvers, like turning and stopping without falling off. Given skateboarding's unsavory reputation, many parents would have discouraged their son from spending so much time doing something considered to be pointless, dangerous, or both. But the Hawks were different. From the very beginning, they supported Tony's interest in skateboarding and encouraged him. "We were just glad that he took his energy out on a skateboard and not us," remembers his mother.

One day the mother of one of Tony's friends took Tony and her son to a nearby skate park called Oasis, one of the few that remained open. Until that time, as Tony remembers, "I thought skateboarding was just a mode of transportation." That day at the skate park changed everything.

He saw skaters going up, down, around, and over the smooth walls of the park's obstacles at tremendous speeds, doing simple spins, jumps, and Ollies — maneuvers that he had never seen before. Other skaters shouted their approval.

Tony was immediately hooked. He was a big fan of the daredevil motorcyclist Evel Knievel, who performed motorcycle jumps off ramps over cars, buses, and other dangerous obstacles. To Tony, skating appeared to be just as thrilling. Tony wanted to be the skater doing the tricks that everyone else watched.

The atmosphere at the skate park also intrigued him. He identified with many of the other skaters. Like Tony, some felt different from other kids and shunned organized sports. At the same time, even though many wore helmets and knee and elbow pads, they appeared fearless and athletic, and skated as if the skateboard was a part of their body. Some sported tattoos and played loud, aggressive rock music on boom boxes while they skated. Everyone at the park had a nickname, and the skaters used slang words that described every trick and maneuver they used while skating. For the first time in his life, Tony Hawk felt as if he belonged.

Tony started taking a bus to the skate park after school and spending hours hanging out and practicing. Every evening, his parents would drive by and pick him up. "We'd have to drag him home," his mother once told a reporter. "He would kick and scream, saying, 'If I do this trick five hundred more times, I can get it!'" On Saturdays and Sundays, Tony often spent the entire day at the park.

But that didn't turn Tony's parents off from the sport. "I think the skate parks were invaluable," his mother said later. "I knew where he was and that he was safe. It gave him the opportunity to do what he loved all day long. We would never let him go out on the streets all day." It helped that there were always adults working at the park, making sure that everyone was safe.

Skateboarding began to take over Tony's life. He started showing up at baseball and basketball practices still wearing his kneepads from the skate park. When he was playing other sports, he still found it hard to concentrate. Now, when he was waiting for something to happen, he inevitably found he was thinking about how to perform a new trick on the skateboard rather than concentrating on hitting the ball or making a shot.

Finally, Tony made a decision. He believed that playing other sports was preventing him from skating as much as he wanted and was holding back his progress. He decided he didn't want to play basketball or baseball anymore.

There was just one problem. Frank Hawk was president of the local Little League. Even though Frank supported his skating, Tony was afraid that if he stopped playing baseball, his dad would be upset with him.

After worrying about his father's reaction for several days, Tony finally mustered the courage to tell him that he didn't want to play other sports. As Tony explained later, it wasn't so much that he didn't like the other sports; he liked skating more. "Every time I went to the skate park," he said, "I would leave thinking I was better than when I came. I never had that feeling playing baseball. And skateboarding was

Tony Hawk preps for a 720 in the halfpipe . . .

catches air and begins his rotation . . .

cranks his upper body around . . .

J. Grant Brittain

follows with his lower body . . .

then gets ready to nail a pinpoint landing!

The skateboard master surveys the scene.

J. Grant Brittain

Defying gravity once . . .

twice . . .

three times!

Tony Hawk does a crooked grind on a rail.

Like father, like son: Riley Hawk jumps over his dad!

Tony Hawk's Competitive History

Date	Event	Location	Discipline	Finish
1999	GlissExpo Festival	Euro Disney, Paris, France	Vert	1
1999	Slam City Jam	Vancouver, BC	Vert	6
1999	X Trials	Richmond, VA	Street	18
1999	X Trials	Richmond, VA	Vert	1
1998	B3	Oceanside, CA	Street	2
1998	B3	Oceanside, CA	Vert	1
1998	B3	Woodward Camp, PA	Street	1
1998	B3	Woodward Camp, PA	Vert	1
1998	Globe Shoes World Cup	Munster, Germany	Vert	1
1998	Spot	Tampa, FL	Vert	1
1998	Triple Crown of Skateboarding	Asbury Park, NJ	Vert	1
1998	Triple Crown of Skateboarding	Overall	Vert	12
1998	World Cup Skateboarding	Overall	Vert	1
1998	X Trials	Virginia Beach, VA	Street	4
1998	X Trials	Virginia Beach, VA	Vert	1
1997	Hard Rock	Hollywood, CA	Vert Overall	2
1997	Hard Rock	Hollywood, CA	Vert	2
1997	Hard Rock	Hollywood, CA	Vert Doubles	1
1997	Vans Generation	London, England	Vert	1
1997	World Cup Skateboarding	Overall	Vert Overall	6
1996	Hard Rock	Hollywood, CA	Vert	2
1996	Hard Rock	Las Vegas, NV	Vert	1
1996	X Trials	Seal Beach, CA	Street	3
1996	X Trials	San Padre, TX	Street	2
1996	X Trials	San Padre, TX	Vert	1

Summer X Games History

Year	Discipline	Finish
1998	Vert	3
1998	Vert Doubles	1
1997	Vert	1
1997	Vert Doubles	1
1996	Street	7
1996	Vert	2
1995	Street	2
1995	Vert	1

such an individual thing. If you messed up, you didn't let the team down."

Frank Hawk surprised his son. He listened patiently to Tony, and then asked him if he was sure about his decision. When Tony said that he was, Frank told his son that if he didn't want to play other sports apart from skating, it was okay. He was just happy that Tony had found something he loved to do.

The parents of some of Tony's friends had a much different reaction. They thought skating was a waste of time and that most skaters were bad people who did drugs and got into a lot of trouble. Some of Tony's friends had to sneak off to the skate park or beg their parents to be allowed to go there.

But the Hawks were much more open-minded. They saw through the rebellious attitude that many skaters adopted and recognized that the vast majority of kids at the park were there because it was the only place they could safely do something they truly loved to do. The Hawks actually encouraged Tony to skate, because they noticed that the more their son skated, the happier he was.

"When he started getting good at skating, it changed his personality," remembers his brother, Steve. "He became a different guy. He was calm, he started thinking about other people and became more generous. He wasn't so worried about losing."

At the time, skateboarding was completely unorganized as a sport. A few companies sponsored a handful of skaters, giving them free equipment and small sums of money to give clinics and exhibitions demonstrating tricks. A few small magazines covered skateboarding and the skateboard culture, but there was no organizing body or standard set of rules by which skaters could compete against one another. And although a few skate parks held their own competitions, each was held according to different rules. Few skaters and even fewer fans were very interested in them.

Frank Hawk sensed an opportunity. He knew there were thousands of kids just like Tony who preferred skateboarding to other sports. But Frank also knew that until skating was organized like other sports, many parents would still be resistant to the sport, and that without goals to achieve some skaters would inevitably abandon skateboarding. Frank

Hawk didn't want that to happen to his son, and he wanted adults to see skating as a positive experience like he did. So he came up with a solution.

Frank Hawk founded the California Amateur Skateboard League, the CASL, a kind of Little League for skateboarders. Frank Hawk learned as much as he could about skating, quizzing Tony and his friends about all the different tricks they did and what made one skater better than another. Then he talked to the skate park operators and skateboard manufacturers, explaining his plans for the sport. There were a few similiar organizations in other parts of the country and Frank researched what they were trying to do, learning from their mistakes.

Eventually the CASL took skateboarding into a new realm. Frank and experienced skaters developed a consistent set of rules to govern competitions, created a method of scoring done by judges trained by Frank, set standards for the various tricks in the sport, and made certain safety equipment, like helmets and knee and elbow pads, mandatory in competition.

At first, Tony and many other skaters weren't sure how they felt about the competitions. Part of what they found attractive about skating was that it wasn't competitive in an organized way. They worried that organized competition might strip the sport of its spontaneity.

But Frank Hawk was sensitive to their concerns and made certain that the CASL recognized what was unique about the sport. Skaters wouldn't be competing against each other as much as they would be competing against themselves. Everyone would simply be trying to improve and reach a higher standard. In a way, the competitions would simply imitate, on a more formal basis, what was happening informally every day at the skate park.

But his father's involvement in the CASL posed a special problem for Tony. While he loved to skate and found that the competitions gave him even more reason to practice, he was uncomfortable with the fact that his father ran the competitions. Like many adolescents, he was a little embarrassed by the attention his father lavished on him, and he was afraid that some skateboarders would think the competitions were set up just for him.

Frank worked hard to try to make sure the competitions were fair, although he admitted later, "I always said I was doing it for other kids, but subconsciously, yes, I was doing it for Tony."

As Steve Hawk later recalled, "At first Tony was embarrassed about winning competitions set up by my father. He was performing on a stage my father built." During a competition, Tony acted as if he didn't even know his father, not talking to him and not even looking in his direction.

There were some awkward moments, as Frank would sometimes forget that he was supposed to be impartial and berate a judge for giving Tony a low score. On one occasion Frank and Tony had a big argument about Frank's involvement in the sport.

But when Frank explained that he had a responsibility to the other kids and couldn't just abandon his position, Tony began to understand. "It was hard for me to do my own thing, the way my dad got so involved," Tony recalled later. "But now I see he was the guy who stepped in and got organized skateboarding started when no one else would. Looking back, I don't understand how he could have been working. He must not have been, with all the hours he spent at the skate park."

Tony rarely questioned his father's motivation

again. Frank Hawk worked tirelessly for the sport, even picking up other skaters and driving them to competitions, then buying everyone dinner afterward. And the other skaters never thought Frank Hawk was being unfair. "It never reflected on me," Tony remembers. "All my friends know my dad is a really cool guy." Over time father and son adjusted to the potential conflict of interest the CASL posed to Tony.

All of the time Tony spent practicing at the skate park began to pay off. Tony did well in CASL competitions, and the other skaters never thought that Tony was getting special treatment or anything. He was just good, and they all knew how much he practiced. Within a year after going to the skate park for the first time, Tony could keep up with the best skaters at the park. By age twelve he was beginning to be recognized as one of the best young skaters in California.

He was different from many of the other skaters. For his age, Tony was tall and thin. Many of the other, more accomplished skaters were much shorter, with low centers of gravity. Shorter skaters generally have an advantage because taller skaters have a high center of gravity, which makes it harder to perform difficult tricks, particularly those that take place in the air.

Tony was able to turn the disadvantage of his height into an advantage. Because he was so tall, he had to practice harder to learn a trick and he had to learn the trick perfectly, making him a technically more accomplished skater. When he finally learned a trick, his larger, more athletic frame sometimes make the trick look more difficult to do than it really was. But his size also helped highlight the tricks and made them look athletic and flamboyant. His background in other sports proved to be an advantage, too, for Tony, despite his size, was better coordinated than many of his peers, most of whom hadn't participated in other sports.

Tony soon began dominating the CASL competitions, winning nearly every time. Most were freestyle competitions, where the skaters propelled themselves around the varying layouts of the skate parks, each of which was different. Some had ramps and bowls that allowed skaters to gain a great deal of speed and launch themselves into the air as if defying gravity. Others formed series of concrete hummocks, wide curves, and other features that mimicked some of the obstacles that skaters often found on the streets, like curbs.

The skaters were allowed a tremendous amount of freedom in their programs. In most instances they were allowed to lay out their own course through the parks, performing both mandatory, standard tricks and other maneuvers limited only by their own sense of invention.

Competition helped skating evolve rapidly, as the skaters pushed one another to keep trying new tricks, sometimes spinning in the air, doing flips, and learning to do them both backward and forward. There was almost no limit to the tricks the skaters came up with using the same few basic moves.

Even then, Tony Hawk was breaking new ground. Many skaters performed their tricks in a haphazard fashion, stringing together tricks with little prior planning. But Tony was different.

He skated strategically, putting a great deal of time and effort into designing a fluid program with a distinctive shape and flow. He tended to start slowly with the more basic moves, then added more difficult tricks as his program progressed, logically moving from one trick to another without stopping or slowing down to regroup, building toward the end of the program. He usually finished with a flourish, saving his most difficult and impressive moves until the end of the program, so they'd still be fresh in the minds of the judges.

In addition to the now-standard Ollie, Tony was performing other tricks like the Kickflip. The Kickflip is much like an Ollie, only instead of placing the front foot on the middle of the nose to stay straight, the skater places it off the corner, allowing the board to spin around in the air, so that when the skater lands he is going backward. Another basic trick off the Ollie is the Nose or Tail Grab, where the skater grabs either the front or back of the board while in midair. But everybody, even Tony Hawk, occasionally and accidentally performed a Wilson, slipping off the skateboard as if it were a banana peel. The Wilson is named after the character Mr. Wilson, who often slips on banana peels in the comic strip "Dennis the Menace."

But unlike many other similar sports, like figure

skating, in which falls are critical errors that usually make it impossible for a skater to win a competition, skateboarding tends to reward accomplishment more than penalize failure. Skateboarders recognize that falls are part of the sport, and in competition a fall can often be overcome by nailing a difficult trick. In fact, playing it safe during a competition, like not trying hard tricks in order not to fall, usually results in a lower score than a more ambitious program that might cause the skater to fall or temporarily lose balance.

Still, falling could lead to injury, something many skate parks were only too aware of. While many skate parks were shutting down over the liability issue, the CASL helped keep the sport going. The organization let manufacturers know that there was still interest in the sport. In response, manufacturers often underwrote the competitions, paying expenses in exchange for the opportunity to display their logos.

When Tony was twelve years old and his reputation was just starting to grow, a skateboard company identified him as one of the sport's next stars. Dogtown, a skateboard manufacturer, decided to sponsor him, giving him free equipment and helping to pay for his expenses as he traveled to different competitions up and down the West Coast. In exchange, Tony agreed to use their equipment and put their logos on his board. Skateboarding was about to take Tony Hawk to places he had never dreamed of.

Chapter Four:

The Sponsored One

At first, Tony didn't see being sponsored as a very big deal and it didn't make much of a difference in the way he viewed skating. He thought it was cool to get free stuff, but he still saw himself as just a kid who loved skating.

But one day, while racing down a narrow curved ramp — known as a "keyhole" — at the Oasis skate park, Tony accidentally collided with another skater named Dave Andrecht, who was several years older and probably the best skater at the park. Like Tony, Andrecht was also sponsored.

Tony took a bad fall and was slammed to the pavement. He was both embarrassed and a little scraped up. As he sat on the ground nursing his wounds, Andrecht stopped to check on him. He noted the tears streaming down Tony's face and said, "You can't cry now. You're sponsored."

Tony stopped sniffling. He tried to act as if he wasn't hurt, jumping back on his board and gliding off to perform another trick. As he did, he realized that everything had changed. He now understood that other skaters were watching every move he made on and off his skateboard. He wasn't just some anonymous kid. Skating wasn't just something he did anymore; it was part of his life. Everything he wanted to achieve in life was centered on skateboarding.

He soon realized that with his talent came a certain measure of responsibility. Other skaters were beginning to look up to him. He noticed that when he tried new tricks, or a series of tricks, other skaters took notice and began to follow suit. He realized that he wasn't in competition *against* the other skaters as much as he was in competition *with* them, as they were all working together for the mutual benefit of everyone who skateboarded.

Tony also noticed that if he dressed a certain way, or listened to certain kinds of music, other skaters soon imitated him. Like many of his fellow skaters, Tony listened to punk rock and wore clothes that reflected the dressed-down, working-class image of the music. Skaters didn't wear uniforms like participants in other sports. They wore sneakers, baggy shorts, and T-shirts. Tony started to live the skaters' life full time.

Tony now admits that he didn't take school as seriously as he should have, saying, "I never imagined any future for myself outside skateboarding." He was smart and was able to get by with little effort, but he viewed school as something to get out of the way so he could spend more time skating. Besides, at school he still felt like an outcast, someone who was different. Even though he was becoming famous in the skateboard world, few kids at school had any appreciation for skateboarders. They were considered strange by many of the kids who played football or were in the marching band or participated in other extracurricular activities.

"I didn't relate to anyone," Tony recalled later. "I never went to a single school function. I was going to school because I had to." Tony just skated. That was his world.

Tony's focus on his sport continued to pay off. His skills began to eclipse those of nearly everyone else at the park. He could do all the tricks the older, more experienced skaters could. Rather than shunning him as some athletes who were jealous of a younger athlete's ability might do, the older skaters sought him out for his company.

It would have been easy for Tony to become satisfied with his stature at Oasis and as one of the best skaters in the CASL. After all, Tony was now an adolescent. He was paying more attention to girls at the skate park, and the girls started to flock to the popular young skateboarder.

But Tony wasn't satisfied. His only competition became himself. He knew that in order to keep improving, he had to become creative and think of new tricks.

Like most sports, almost every skateboard move stems from a few fundamental movements. Tony became a master at putting several fundamental movements together to create something that hadn't been done before in that combination, like adding a flip or twisting his body around as if his feet were attached to the board. In fact, Tony has probably created more tricks than anyone else in the history of skating. He has invented so many that he's even lost count, sheepishly admitting that he has invented "at least fifty" different tricks.

One of the cool things about inventing a trick is that the inventor usually gets to name the trick. Tony became a master at creating and using skateboard slang to describe his various maneuvers, like an Ollie 540, in which he performs an Ollie and spins around one and a half times without holding on to the board. Other signature tricks have such inventive names as the 360 Kickflip Mute Grab, the Madonna, the Varial 540, and the Popshuvit Nosegrind. Many of the most common terms that refer to skateboarding tricks today were actually created by Tony Hawk years ago.

As much as Tony enjoyed skating in the CASL, after a couple years he began looking ahead to greater challenges. Frank Hawk stepped in once more.

Professional skateboarding had a checkered past. The few sponsored skaters competed in a handful of events that were often sponsored by those same companies. These were usually vert competitions held in pools or skate park bowls that mimicked pool conditions. But there was little money involved, and the fact that the competitions were sponsored by skateboard manufacturers made some people question their impartiality, as they rewarded skaters who simply blasted around bowls and over the concrete lips of swimming pools. Other, more inventive, skating styles were ignored.

Although Tony Hawk had participated in some pro-am events, the experience hadn't been a positive one. The pro skaters dismissed his gawky style, which concentrated on spins and flips, even laughing behind his back.

Frank Hawk realized his son was dissatisfied. He sensed another opportunity. He created the National Skateboarding Association, the first organized professional skateboarding circuit, to build upon what he'd started in the CASL.

At age fourteen, Tony Hawk turned pro.

Chapter Five:

A Star Is Born

Today, if a skater is talented enough to turn professional, chances are that although he or she may be able to earn a modest living, only a chosen few earn in excess of one hundred thousand dollars a year. Skaters earn money for endorsing various skateboard products, ranging from boards to clothing and shoes, and from sponsors, who will pay the skater a fee to display their logos on their skateboards and make appearances on behalf of the company.

Another source of income is from competitions, like the X Games. Just like in other sports, professional skaters compete against one another for money.

Yet another source of income for the professional skater comes from the sale of videos. A skater with a great reputation can star in a video in which he or she demonstrates his or her best tricks, often to a raucous rock music accompaniment, creatively shot by videographers who are big skateboard fans. The most popular videos of this kind can sell hundreds of thousands of copies and earn the performers a lot of money.

It hadn't been like this when Tony Hawk turned pro. Even though Frank Hawk's organizational genius soon made NSA-sponsored events the only ones that mattered, there still wasn't a great deal of money in pro skateboarding. When Tony Hawk began competing in the NSA, he was usually skating for equipment and a hundred dollars or so per event.

But ever so slowly, NSA competitions stimulated interest in the sport that previous professional competitions had failed to, for the NSA, like the CASL, designed competitions that recognized the uniqueness of skateboarding. They didn't treat it like a combination between roller-skating, ice-skating, surfing, and skiing.

The NSA also helped provide a middle ground where various skating styles overlapped and came together, as it recognized both street style skating and the more straightforward approach of competitive skateboarding that had its beginnings in the CASL.

A handful of publications, like *Thrasher*, popped up, giving skateboarding and skateboard culture a much-needed boost. Younger kids, many of whom had never skateboarded before, were first drawn into the sport by the magazines. And the magazines, in turn, gave skateboard manufacturers a place to advertise and promote the sport.

But more than anything else, skateboarding needed a star, someone whose talent, ability, and charisma could earn the respect of everyone interested in skating as well as draw new people to the sport. Tony Hawk quickly became that star.

He had grown up, both physically and emotionally. Although he was still rail-thin, Hawk was strong, and six feet tall and getting taller, making everything he did on a skateboard appear increasingly athletic.

He was also smart enough to stay out of the occasional spats between different skating factions. Street skaters respected him for his daring and his ability to do tricks no other skater had thought of before, while competitive skaters began to appreciate his technical skill and artistry. At the same time, Hawk shared the interest many street skaters had for punk rock and the punk attitude, yet he still approached skating with the seriousness and dedication admired by the sport's competitive side. In the skateboarding world, he was the equivalent of a Babe Ruth in baseball or a Michael Jordan in basketball. He brought everyone together and took the sport into a new era.

At age fourteen, Hawk was suddenly rated as the best skateboarder in the world. He began to dominate NSA events, just as he had in the CASL a few years earlier. His dominance, in turn, pushed other skaters like Christian Hosoi and Steve Caballero to new levels.

That was only one of the changes taking place in Tony's life. His family moved from Carlsbad to Cardiff, California, closer to San Diego, where Hawk attended and eventually graduated from Torrey Pines High School. Fortunately for Tony, the new home was also closer to a skate park, the Del Mar Surf and Turf, where Hawk was soon a frequent visitor.

The move came at the perfect time for Hawk. He didn't have to take the bus to the park and then wait for his parents to pick him up anymore. The park was near enough to his house that he could go there to train and practice anytime he wanted.

Hawk took full advantage of his proximity to the park, and his skills improved rapidly. When he practiced, he usually did so at marathon sessions lasting as long as three or four hours. To the other skaters at the park, it sometimes seemed as if Hawk was coming up with a brand-new trick that no one else had even thought of, much less done, every three or four weeks.

He became the first skater ever to launch his board out of a pool with the force of his body alone. Until Tony came along, the only way skaters were able to jump out of the pool was by going up and down one side and then the other over and over again, slowly building speed and momentum until they were able to get in the air. Hawk, by using his body and working with centrifugal force, was able to get into the air on his first attempt.

It was an enormous breakthrough, for as other skaters learned Hawk's technique, vert competitions became non-stop, action-filled events. Now skaters could string together as many as sixteen or seventeen tricks in the fifty-second time limit, virtually a trick every time they went up or down the bowl.

One skateboarding observer accurately called Hawk "the future of skateboarding." But thus far, the only people who could see the future were those who shared the skate parks and pools with Tony Hawk.

That was all about to change.

Chapter Six:

Ups and Downs on the Halfpipe

It is difficult to say whether Tony Hawk came to professional skateboarding at the perfect time for professional skateboarding or whether professional skateboarding came into existence at the perfect time for Tony Hawk. And it really doesn't matter, for the end results would be identical. Hawk and pro skateboarding were made for each other.

A Tony Hawk victory in NSA competition became almost a foregone conclusion, as he swept and rolled and spun to victory in nearly three out of every four competitions. But just as his career began to take off, he was rocked by a family tragedy. One evening when Tony was alone with his father, Frank Hawk had a heart attack. Tony quickly called an ambulance.

As he waited for help to arrive, his father's life

hanging in the balance, Hawk began to recognize all the sacrifices his parents had made for him. Fortunately, his father recovered, but the incident brought the two closer than they'd ever been before.

It may have been a coincidence, or just the result of growing up, but after his father's heart attack Hawk became even more dominant on the NSA circuit. His performance led to a sponsorship deal with Powell Peralta, a leading manufacturer of skateboard equipment and apparel. Hawk became the best known member of the "Bones Brigade," a team of skaters all sponsored by Peralta.

The Bones Brigade dominated every competition. Hawk usually finished in first place as other team members fought for second or third.

Hawk's breakthrough style, which appeared to be equal parts daredevil, gymnast, acrobat, and ballet dancer, sparked a skateboard revival. When Peralta decided to manufacture a Tony Hawk signature skateboard in 1986, they sold as many as 20,000 boards a month. Tony Hawk received a dollar for each board sold.

At about the same time, Stacy Peralta produced a

skateboarding documentary film entitled *The Search for Animal Chin,* starring Hawk and other cutting-edge skateboarders.

The video, which was shot at a brand-new park built for Peralta that featured a double halfpipe, provided the perfect forum to spread the legend of Tony Hawk all across the world. Before the video, many skateboarders had only been able to read about Tony Hawk and look at still photographs of him in action. The video changed all that.

Now fans could see Hawk do things they had only dreamed were possible. He seemed to defy gravity as he launched himself into an Ollie an incredible six or eight feet into the air above the halfpipe. This provided enough height to allow him to perform an unbelievable variety of maneuvers in seemingly endless combinations. He sometimes twisted either to his frontside or backside, while other times he'd spin horizontally a full 360 or even 540 degrees. Other times he turned somersaults, referred to in skateboarding as flips, grabbing his board with one hand and sometimes doing handstands called inverts, on the coping (the edge of the pipe) with his free hand. Then, as gravity took hold and brought him back toward earth, he would land the board squarely on the uppermost portion of the halfpipe, pointing at a ninety-degree angle to the ground. He would rocket down at full speed either forward or backward to the other side of the pipe and launch himself in the air again to perform yet another trick. Hawk was able to string these tricks together seamlessly and make it all look almost effortless.

The variations Hawk was able to accomplish were mind-boggling, limited only by his own imagination. He would try a trick frontside, turning in the direction he was facing, and then backside, turning blindly to the rear. Or his tricks could end or begin in a revert, with Hawk moving backward.

The video was a huge success, and almost overnight Tony Hawk became the biggest name ever in skateboarding — throughout the world. Vert skating, Hawk's specialty, became the most popular form of skateboard competition. All over the country kids began building their own ramps so they could try to mimic Hawk's gravity-defying tricks. Other businesses took note of Hawk's surging popularity and were eager to use him to reach the lucrative youth market. All of a sudden, he began making appearances in all sorts of ads, both for skateboard products and for mainstream products like soft drinks. He even made a movie, appearing as a skateboarding pizza delivery boy in 1987's *Gleaming the Cube*, starring Christian Slater. Everyone wanted Hawk to appear in their skateboarding video.

Hawk's life was changing rapidly. In a period of only a few years he went from being a kid who skated to one of the best-known skateboarders in the world, known by his nickname, "Birdman." Even though he was still in high school, where many of his classmates still considered him some kind of weirdo skater outcast, he began earning a tremendous amount of money. From 1983 to 1987, skateboarding went from a 4-million-dollar hobby to a 300-million-dollar industry. No skater was in a better position to take advantage of the growth of skateboarding than Tony Hawk was. In fact, he was singularly responsible for much of it.

In 1986 alone, when Hawk was only eighteen years old and in the process of graduating from high school, he earned over $100,000 — $10,000 in prize money in competition and the rest from videos, endorsements, exhibitions, and stunt work in movies like *Police Academy IV.* Wherever he went, he wowed crowds with what became his most famous trick — a 720, in which he was able to do two complete flips.

It was a heady time for the young superstar. Long feature articles on him appeared in magazines like *Sports Illustrated* and *People,* and he was regularly profiled in skateboard magazines. At his father's suggestion, he bought a house back in his old hometown of Carlsbad for $124,000, which he shared with several skateboarding buddies. It was a teenager's dream, with a Jacuzzi, tons of stereo equipment, and an outdoor gazebo. He soon married a young woman named Cindy, whom he had met at a local mall.

Hawk's life went into the fast lane. He traveled almost nonstop all around the world from one competition to another, squeezing in videos and other works whenever he could. The NSA expanded operations and began to sponsor competitions in Europe and Japan, with first-place prize money sometimes approaching $10,000. Life was so good Hawk even bought a second house out in the country.

In many ways, Hawk was living a life many of his

peers could only dream of. He was rich — and skateboarding for a living. As he later told a reporter, "That was a great time for us. We were making a ton of money and we flew all over the world." In skating slang, Hawk and the other premier skaters were "stoked." As one observer noted, Hawk and a few other skaters were "living like rock stars."

But everything wasn't perfect in Tony Hawk's world. His sudden fame held him to a different standard. At NSA competitions, judges expected him to be perfect. When he wasn't, he was penalized for small mistakes far more harshly than other skaters. He started to become disenchanted with competitive skateboarding.

Hawk wasn't alone. Although skateboarding had boomed throughout the late 1980s, there were still precious few places for skaters to skate. That didn't stop skaters, of course. They simply took to the street.

A new style of street skating began to emerge, one that took advantage of the technical leaps made by Hawk and others and put them into practice on the street. Vert skating began to be considered out of style as street skaters turned stairs, park benches, railings, and other commonplace obstacles into their preferred places to skate. Many street skaters looked down on organized skateboarding competitions, just as Tony Hawk had once looked down on other organized sports when he was first starting to skate. Street skaters looked at Hawk and other established vert skaters as old-fashioned and out of touch, what they called "old school." Younger skaters were drawn to street skating as skateboard magazines focused on the emerging style. The money in vert skating, from sponsors, competitions, and videos, began to dry up as manufacturers began to court a new generation of skaters. The skating community began to split into different factions again.

At the same time, skateboarding received a lot of bad publicity. Several once-famous skaters got in serious legal trouble, much of it due to their abuse of drugs and alcohol, and one well-known skater was even imprisoned after killing his girlfriend. Such behavior really had nothing to do with skateboarding, but the image of the sport still suffered.

Skateboarding also faced a challenge from some new technology. Inline skates were invented and suddenly became very popular. Just as skateboarding had evolved by combining elements of both roller-skating and surfing, inline skating combined roller-skating and skateboarding. Inline skaters even developed styles similar to skateboarding, as inline skaters practiced both street-style skating and vert skating. Some skateboarders put their skateboards in the closet and bought inline skates, and many kids who had never experienced either sport before chose inline skating over skateboarding.

Although Hawk was so talented that he was one of the few vert skaters who could also skate street style, he wasn't the new, hot, young skater anymore. Barely twenty years old, he was in danger of becoming a has-been. After soaring into the air, Tony Hawk was plummeting back to earth.

Chapter Seven:

Getting Down to Business

As the decade of the 1980s ended and the 1990s began, Tony Hawk was in free fall. In only a few short years he went from being the skater everyone looked up to to becoming someone who *used* to be somebody. For a while, he even considered quitting competitive skateboarding altogether. "I had done it so long and had reached the level I wanted to reach," he later recalled. There appeared to be little more left to accomplish, and as Tony himself said, "It wasn't fun anymore."

It also wasn't very lucrative. Hawk's skating income dried up almost completely. Cindy went to work as a manicurist, and Hawk had to ask his wife for spending money just to keep gas in his beat-up old Honda Civic and to get a bite to eat. His old friends called it his "Taco Bell money," after the fast-food restaurant Hawk often dined at.

He wasn't quite sure what to do. He'd given up on the idea of going to college years earlier, and had never cared for school anyway. But somehow, some way, he knew he wanted to stay involved with skateboarding.

A Swedish skater named Per Welinder provided the solution. Welinder had a business background and talked Hawk into becoming his partner in a skateboard company. Since the rise of street style, most board companies had marketed their products by flaunting the skating lifestyle, concentrating on its most rebellious, antiestablishment elements. They didn't bother using individual skaters to represent their boards.

Hawk and Welinder thought this was misguided. They had seen the cyclical rise and fall of skating before and they refused to believe that vert skating was dead forever. They believed that if they created their own team, led by Hawk, they could revive vert skating and use their team to promote their own line of skateboards.

There was just one problem. Welinder figured

that the two skaters would need $100,000 to get their company, which they decided to call "Birdhouse" after Hawk, off the ground. Welinder had his share. Hawk didn't.

But he did have his two houses. He sold his country house and took a second mortgage out on the house in Carlsbad. "Here was everything I'd worked for all my life," he said later. "And I was willing to drop it all into one last stab at things."

It was a tremendous gamble. Most new businesses fail, and Hawk was dumping his life savings into skateboarding, a business that many believed was on its way out. Moreover, he had absolutely no experience in the business world. He hadn't even saved very much of the many hundred thousand dollars he had earned in skating. If the business collapsed, he'd lose what little remained.

But Tony Hawk had never played it safe. On many occasions he'd described his skating philosophy by saying, "I never go halfway. If I don't do my best, it eats at me. It kills me inside." He approached the business the same way.

Hawk and Welinder worked doggedly at building their business. They knew skateboarding, so they knew what skaters wanted in a product, and Hawk's name still carried some weight in skating circles. He continued to skate competitively whenever he could, knowing that he had to keep performing in order to maintain his credibility. He remained a fixture at skate parks throughout Southern California and traveled to other parks throughout the country demonstrating his Birdhouse boards.

Yet all the hours he spent on the business were hard on his marriage. Even though Cindy gave birth to a son, Riley, she and Tony began to drift apart.

But Hawk was determined to make it. The kid who couldn't focus became single-minded when it came down to the success of his company.

Birdhouse also got lucky. After scraping by for a few years, they were able to take advantage of a new generation of skaters who weren't as concerned with whether vert skaters or street skaters were cooler than the other was. They just liked to skate, and appreciated both styles.

Hawk believed that in order to grow, skateboarding had to change its image. As long as people thought of skateboarding as a dangerous pastime and skateboarders as a bunch of juvenile delinquents, he knew the sport would have a hard time continuing to grow. If parents refused to allow their kids to skateboard, there was simply no way for the sport to expand.

"What so many people don't understand," Hawk once explained, "is that kids wouldn't be out there on the street carving up curbs and park benches if they'd just provide them someplace to skate." So Hawk became something of an ambassador for the sport.

Wherever he went, he was unfailingly polite, signing autographs and talking with kids, telling them to make sure they always wore their safety equipment, handing out stickers, showing young skaters and their parents that skaters and skateboarding weren't anything to be afraid of. Although when he was on a skateboard he performed the most difficult stunts imaginable and was as radical and daring as any skater in the world, off the board he could be a soft-spoken businessman and father who loved spending time with his son and just chilling out.

Hawk didn't see any conflict between the two images. Both were real and genuine, because that's who Tony Hawk was. He had matured. Hawk had been skating long enough to know that being a great skater had nothing to do with the kind of clothes he wore or the kind of music he listened to. And being a businessman and a good father didn't mean he still couldn't be one of the greatest skateboarders in the world. He was still getting better every day, as a skater, as a businessman, and, just as importantly, as a person.

A decade before, skating had needed Tony Hawk to become its first superstar in order to grow. Now, it needed him to become its first role model. He would soon prove as adept in his new role as he had been, and continued to be, in the first.

Chapter Eight:

Extremely Popular

By 1995, Birdhouse had established itself in the highly competitive business of skateboard manufacturing. Hawk wasn't making a fortune, but he was getting by. Although vert skating still lagged behind street style in terms of popularity, it hadn't disappeared. And as more kids started skating and the long-time problems associated with skating in public places resurfaced, people began building skateboard parks again. Fortunately for the sport, some changes in the laws made it possible to run a skate park without spending so much on insurance. And increasingly, some communities were showing their willingness to build skate parks themselves, as people who had once been skaters had now grown up and started taking an interest in the way skating was viewed where they lived.

For Tony Hawk, it was a time of highs and lows. He divorced Cindy and took responsibility for the end of his marriage, admitting he spent too much time on the road, away from his wife. But the two agreed to the joint custody of their son, Riley, and Hawk found that he enjoyed being a father. At age three, Riley could already do an Ollie, and Hawk found himself behaving toward his son much the same way his own father had behaved toward Tony. The two spent hours playing together, even playing basketball and baseball. Hawk's life had come nearly full circle.

Then Tony's father got sick. In March of 1995, Frank Hawk was diagnosed with lung cancer, and his condition quickly deteriorated. In July he passed away.

Tony was greatly saddened by his death, but it made him feel better knowing that he and his father had been closer than most fathers and sons, and his relationship with Riley helped heal his loss. Several hundred people attended Frank Hawk's funeral, as the entire skateboarding community turned out to honor him.

In the meantime Hawk kept trying to learn new tricks. With the 720 out of the way, most skaters considered Hawk's Kickflip McTwist, a move in which he flips his board with his feet while spinning his body 540 degrees in the air, as the most difficult trick. But Hawk wasn't satisfied. He set his sights on skateboarding's Holy Grail, a trick that everyone talked about but no one, anywhere, had ever been able to do. The trick was known simply as the 900, an incredible two and a half flips off the halfpipe.

Even the most talented skaters considered the trick virtually impossible. In order to somersault a full two-and-a-half rotations in the air before landing, a skater had to achieve incredible height — at least eight feet above the usual eleven-foot height of the halfpipe — which meant that the fall back down to land in the pipe approached twenty feet. Falling from such a height was dangerous, and even if the trick was nailed, the skater's body would still suffer from an incredible pounding. Halfpipes aren't padded, and skateboards don't bounce. Besides, achieving any new trick takes hundreds and hundreds of practice attempts, and missing a 900 was even more dangerous than making one, no matter how much padding and protective equipment the skater wore.

Hawk had tried to do a 900 as far back as 1986, but as he described it, "I could never commit to the spin." In the 900 the skater is blind twice, losing complete sight of the ramp. As much as Hawk wanted to do the trick, his body balked at losing sight of the ramp twice.

And that didn't even take into consideration the difficulty the landing posed. Even if he made the two-and-a-half flips, he would still have to land upright on the board and maintain his balance, a near impossibility after spinning so fast. If he landed short, too long, or not square on his board, serious injury was a real possibility.

Still, every so often Hawk gave it a try. In 1995 he actually accomplished the spin part of the 900 for the first time, but his landing was a disaster, as he cracked his shins on the vert deck. Later, another attempt left him with a cracked rib that knocked him out of competition for several months. After that, Hawk put the 900 out his mind for a while, saying bluntly, "I'm afraid to do 900s."

But early in 1995 Hawk began to hear about a brand-new competition. The Entertainment Sports Network, better known as the television network ESPN, was always on the lookout for new programming. They broadcast all kinds of different sports, from mainstream sports like baseball, football, hockey, auto racing, and basketball, to less popular sports like rodeo and weight lifting and even more obscure events like billiards and cheerleading competitions. ESPN broadcast twenty-four hours a day, seven days a week, and their constant challenge was to come up with enough programming to keep the interest of their audience.

The programmers at ESPN were particularly interested in attracting young male viewers between the ages of twelve and thirty-four. This group is very attractive to advertisers, because they have a lot of money to spend.

But little of ESPN's existing programming took aim at this market. So ESPN decided to create programming that catered to this audience, which the media had dubbed "Generation X."

ESPN knew that new sports like inline skating and mountain biking, alternative sports like snowboarding and skateboarding, and adventurous, extreme sports like climbing were all very popular with this age group. But in many cases, people who participated in one of these alternative sports knew little about the others.

ESPN decided to package all the sports together in one big program, based on a format similar to the Olympic Games, which they decided to call the "Extreme Games." In the Games, various competitors from all around the world would compete in one location over a week or so for medals in the various events. ESPN would then broadcast the competition on their network.

Before the Extreme Games, which were later renamed the X Games, skateboarding and the other sports rarely appeared on broadcast television. ESPN planned to promote the games heavily and hoped to change that. They hoped that once people were exposed to so-called extreme sports, viewers would become fans.

This was big news in the skateboarding community. Never before had the sport been offered the opportunity to reach such a wide audience.

As ESPN began planning the Games, which they

decided to hold in Newport, Rhode Island, Hawk learned that one of the skateboarding events would be the vert. And Hawk was asked to compete.

He jumped at the chance, sensing that perhaps the X Games could help skateboarding enter another period of expansion. The Games had the potential to provide Hawk with the perfect forum to advance the sport.

But not everyone was so thrilled. Some skaters thought a big competition on television would be bad for skating, which they thought should stay closer to its outlaw, street roots. And the mainstream sports media laughed at the idea of people actually watching athletes they'd never heard of compete in sports they'd never seen before. Even Hawk was skeptical, but he also knew that even if the X Games weren't ultimately successful, it was still the biggest skateboard competition that had ever taken place.

The Games were held in midsummer and proved more successful than even ESPN had hoped. Nearly 200,000 spectators turned out to watch the various events, which ranged from sports like the street luge to sky surfing. To capture the excitement of these new sports, ESPN shot them from weird angles and most took place to a raucous soundtrack of rock music.

The vert competition was one of the big hits of the Games. Not only did Tony win, finishing ahead of second-place finisher Andy McDonald, but the vert competition looked great on television. Viewers were thrilled as they saw Hawk soar high above the halfpipe and perform his signature moves. They didn't care that he was almost twice as old as many of the other competitors. His second-place finish in the street competition silenced critics who claimed he could no longer compete with skating's younger stars.

But they also saw the other side of Tony Hawk. He was the subject of a personal feature that showed him as a father and a businessman, well-spoken, polite, grown-up — and still the sickest skater around.

To the general public, the notion that the greatest skateboarder in the world could also be a regular person was a revelation. The X Games marked a turnaround for the sport, at once making it both more popular and, just as important, more acceptable. As one observer later noted, the Games showed "forty-year-old dads why their son isn't picking up a baseball glove anymore."

Even Hawk was stunned by the impact of the competition. Before the X Games, strangers would occasionally ask him what he did for a living. When he responded, "I'm a professional skateboarder," they usually looked at him like he was crazy. They couldn't believe that anyone could actually skateboard for a living.

But when he told people what he did after the Games, they responded to him with a glimmer of recognition, asking him, "Were you that guy I saw in the X Games?" Moreover, even people who had never picked up a skateboard before asked him about the details of his sport, like how much he practiced and how long he'd been skating.

The Games also gave new life to vert competitions. While the street skating fans still enjoyed the freestyle competition, and the downhill race was entertaining, general sports fans found vert the most exciting sport. It was just a lot more interesting to watch.

The Birdman, in one fell swoop, had not only helped spark a revival of his sport but had resumed his place as the best skateboarder in the world. As one street skater later commented, "The image of Tony Hawk is not so hard-core, but that guy, his level of skating is so ridiculous."

Chapter Nine:

Nailing the 900

Both professionally and personally, Tony Hawk was perfectly positioned to take advantage of the next wave in skating's popularity following the inaugural X Games. Sales of Birdhouse products took off, and Hawk found himself in demand as never before. He made several ads for a variety of products and had to sort through a host of offers to appear in videos. Birdhouse even added a clothing line, Hawk Clothing. With the growth of the Internet, Hawk's profile increased further as he set up his own Web site, as well as one for Birdhouse.

The X Games grew each year and with them, so did Tony Hawk's reputation. In 1996 he finished second in the vert and a disappointing seventh in street, but in 1997 he rebounded in magnificent fashion.

Critics had begun to whisper that Hawk was getting old and finally slowing down. And he did decide not to compete in street. There were just too many demands on his time. So he decided to focus on his specialty, the vert. Still, Andy McDonald, the defending champion, was favored to win.

Hawk responded to the added pressure to win. In his final run he nailed all seventeen of his tricks, including a spectacular Varial Heel Flip Lien Grab in which he kicked his board upside down, spun it 180 degrees, then grabbed it with his right hand before landing. He left the other competitors shaking their heads and calling his performance the greatest skateboard show ever.

Afterward when someone asked him how he felt as an old skateboarder of twenty-nine, Hawk quipped, "I don't think about my age when I skate. I feel young. All my tricks felt right-on when I was doing them. I was so nervous and excited that all my emotions just became a wave of calm."

But Hawk wasn't done. The X Games had added a new competition, the vert doubles. In doubles two skaters perform on the same halfpipe, each performing tricks as they cross paths over and over again.

In order to be successful, their timing must be perfect. If either skater is off, they are destined to collide. Each must trust the other completely.

But perhaps no other skate competition demonstrates the unique nature of skateboarders — because in vert doubles Hawk teamed with Andy McDonald, his closest competition in the vert! The two worked together beautifully and captured another gold medal.

With the success of the X Games, other competitions began to take advantage of the incredible surge of popularity in skating. Dozens of skaters were now able to pursue professional careers, and the competition improved dramatically.

Everything was going great for Hawk. He married a former ice-skater named Erin, and the two started their own family when their daughter, Spencer, was born in 1998. ESPN began to utilize him as an announcer covering the Winter X Games and summer qualifier. He took some time to help create a video game, Tony Hawk's Pro Skater, and made plans to create a skate video entitled *The End*. And to top it all off, at the 1998 X Games he collected another gold medal in vert doubles and a bronze in vert.

But something was still gnawing at Tony Hawk. As much as he had accomplished in skating and in business, there was something missing. Of the dozens of tricks he was credited with inventing, from the Ollie 540 to the 360 Kickflip Mute Grab to the Varial 540 and the Popshuvit Nosegrind, one trick had always eluded him.

The 900.

He thought he might be able to pull it off in his video and even built a special oversized ramp that he thought might help. But after trying the 900 dozens of times over a period of several days, he finally gave up, exhausted, saying, "I just couldn't get myself to commit to it." But he wasn't quite ready to give up on the idea of performing the 900.

He got another chance at the 1999 X Games. At the end of the skateboard competitions, ESPN invited Hawk and the four other top vert competitors — Colin McKay, Andy McDonald, Bob Burnquist, and Bucky Lasek — to skate in a twenty-minute "best trick" competition, sort of a skateboarding version of the NBA's slam dunk contest.

The crowd in San Francisco, the site of the competition, was stoked. They had to wait over an hour for the competition to begin because of some technical problems, and got so rowdy that Games officials nearly canceled the contest.

But when the skaters finally began to compete, the atmosphere was electric. Each skater was determined to do his best. Everyone was performing well, yet no one stood out in the first half of the contest. Finally, Andy McDonald nailed a series of difficult tricks, winning over the crowd, and, apparently, the competition. Then Colin McKay did the same. Time was running out for Tony Hawk.

As the clock ticked down and the other competitors slowed, Hawk seemed energized. He paused at the top of the ramp, then shot down and then up the other side before flipping in the air.

He was trying the 900!

He spun in a blur and then crashed down. He'd missed it, but he got right back up and poised on the lip of the ramp and tried again.

He failed again, but by now both the crowd and the other skaters were aware of what he was trying to do. The crowd started rhythmically chanting, "Nine hundred! Nine hundred! Nine hundred!" over and over again as Lasek, McDonald, Burnquist, and McKay cleared out of the way, giving Hawk room and making it possible for him to squeeze in a few more attempts before the end of the 20-minute time period.

Over and over again Hawk launched himself into the air, then tucked and spun faster than seemed humanly possible before dropping out of the sky. Sometimes he pulled out early. Other times, he nailed the spin but crashed upon landing, coming close, but not quite pulling the trick off.

Then, suddenly, the time was up. The competition was over!

Or was it? The crowd began to boo and hoot, and the public address announcer, overcome with excitement, shouted into his microphone, "This is the X Games. We make up the rules as we go along. Let's give him another try!"

The crowd roared in approval, as did the four other skaters. The chant of "Nine hundred! Nine hundred!" began again.

Once more Hawk poised at the top of the ramp and once more he roared to the other side, spun, and dropped. He had the spin down, but kept missing on his landing.

Yet, incredibly, he seemed to be getting stronger. At a time when most skaters would be gasping for breath, Hawk was getting ready to fly.

The crowd wouldn't let him stop and neither would the other skaters, who sat on the edge of the ramp banging their boards in concert with the screaming crowd. And Tony Hawk himself refused to give up. As he told a reporter later, "I just figured I was either going to land it or I was going to wake up later in the hospital."

He tried several more times. The first 900 hung tantalizingly close. Twice he landed on the board only to have it scoot out from under him. Then he climbed the stairs to the top of the halfpipe for the eleventh time.

Again he paused before rocketing down and then up. Again he launched himself into the air, no longer the unsure, frustrated young kid he had been before he ever stepped foot on a skateboard, but a confident man in complete control.

He spun, once, twice, then halfway around again before stretching his body back out and dropping down.

"Thwack!" The sound of Hawk and his board

landing on the ramp resounded through the air as the crowd momentarily stilled as everyone held their breath.

Then as the board shot off, Hawk teetered and tottered for a moment like he had his very first time on the board, frantically windmilling his arms and twisting and turning, trying to keep his balance, his hand momentarily brushing the ramp before he stood, upright and alone for a second, squarely on the board, the Birdman on his perch. Then the crowd went insane and he was engulfed by all sorts and manner of skateboarders.

He had done it!

"This is the greatest day of my life," he shouted to no one in particular and everyone. "The best moment of all time." Other skaters were almost speechless, hardly believing what they had just seen. When a reporter asked Andy McDonald what his best trick had been that day, he just laughed and shook his head, explaining to the puzzled reporter, "It doesn't matter." Because Tony Hawk had just made history.

News of Hawk's accomplishment traveled fast, and it was shown on sports and news programs all over the world. Skateboarding had arrived.

And Tony Hawk, its first superstar, best role model, and greatest champion, knew what to do next.

He retired from competition at the top of his game, but decided to remain heavily involved in skating, announcing, running his company, giving demonstrations, and teaching skateboarding to his children.

Skateboarding had taken him to the top. There was no reason for the Birdman to come back down again.

A Skating Glossary

Skateboarders have developed their own special language, or "slang," to describe their sport. Here are some of the most basic terms used by skateboarders.

air: riding in the air with all four wheels off the ground

backside: a trick or turn done with the skater's back facing the ramp or obstacle

bail: falling on purpose to avoid an out-of-control fall

Caballerial: a 360-degree turn performed on a ramp while riding backward (fakie)

carve: to skate in a long, curving arc

centripetal force: the force that keeps an object, like a skater, moving in a circular path

concave: the inward curve on a skateboard

coping: the material used on the lip of a ramp or bowl, enabling skaters to grind

deck: the flat standing surface of a skateboard, usually made of several layers of maple

fakie: skating backward

frontside: a trick or turn done with the skater's body facing the ramp or obstacle

goofy foot: skating with the right foot on the front of the board; most skaters place their left foot forward

grind: scraping one or both axles on a curb, railing, or other surface

50-50 grind: grinding on both trucks

5-0 grind: grinding on only the back truck

grip tape: sandpaper tape attached to the top of the deck to provide friction, making it easier for the skater to stay on the board

halfpipe: A U-shaped ramp of any size

hang: catching the back wheel on the coping of a ramp

Kickflip: making the board spin after doing an Ollie

McTwist: a 540-degree turn (one-and-a-half revolutions) performed on a ramp

mongo foot: pushing the board with the front foot instead of the back

Nollie: an Ollie done by tapping the nose of the board instead of the tail

nose: the front end of the skateboard

Nosegrind: grinding on only the front truck

Noseslide: sliding the bottom of the nose end of a board on a ledge

Ollie: the most basic trick, a jump made by tapping the tail of the board on the ground

radical: a term used in the 1970s and 1980s meaning "really good"

rail: the outside edge of the skateboard and the plastic strips on the underside of the deck

Railslide: a trick in which the skater slides the bottom of the deck along an object

regular foot: skating with the left foot forward

revert: continuing a trick until the skater and board are going backward

shove-it: spinning the board 180 degrees beneath the feet while traveling forward

sick: the term currently used that means "really good"

slam: an unexpected fall

stoked: pumped up or excited by skating

street skating: skating on streets, curbs, benches, handrails, and other public spaces

switch stance: switching from "goofy foot" to "regular foot" or vice versa

tail: the rear end of the skateboard

Tailslide: sliding the bottom of the tail end of a board on a ledge or lip

trucks: the metal devices in the front and rear that connect the wheels to the deck

vert skating: skating on ramps and other vertical structures specifically designed for skating

vert ramp: a halfpipe, usually at least eight feet tall, with steep sides perfectly vertical near the top

wheelbase: the distance between the front and back wheels

wheelie: balancing the skateboard on two wheels while moving

wheels: the wheels of a skateboard, usually made of polyurethane

The #1
Sports Series
for Kids

Read them all!

All available in paperback from Little, Brown and Company

Matt Christopher®

Kobe Bryant

Terrell Davis

Julie Foudy

Jeff Gordon

Wayne Gretzky

Ken Griffey Jr.

Mia Hamm

Tony Hawk

Grant Hill

Derek Jeter

Randy Johnson

Michael Jordan

Mario Lemieux

Tara Lipinski

Mark McGwire

Greg Maddux

Hakeem Olajuwon

Alex Rodriguez

Briana Scurry

Sammy Sosa

Venus and
Serena Williams

Tiger Woods

Steve Young